LIVING PRAYERS

Our God is one God in Three Persons. All our prayers are offered to the Blessed Trinity— usually to the Father, through the Son, in the Holy Spirit.

Living Prayers

TRADITIONAL AND CONTEMPORARY PRAYERS TO HELP YOUNG CATHOLICS ACHIEVE A DEEPER AND MORE LIVING SPIRITUAL LIFE

By
REV. BASIL SENGER, O.S.B.

Illustrated

CATHOLIC BOOK PUBLISHING CO.
New York

NIHIL OBSTAT: Daniel V. Flynn, J.C.D.
Censor Librorum

IMPRIMATUR: ✠ Joseph T. O'Keefe, D.D.
Administrator, Archdiocese of New York

(T-915)

© 1984 Catholic Book Publishing Co., N.Y.
Printed in Canada

CONTENTS

Foreword

Today many Catholics are seeking ways to pray. They are convinced more than ever that they need to pray. As the Second Vatican Council has stated: "The spiritual life is not limited solely to participation in the Liturgy. The Christian is indeed called to pray with his brothers and sisters, but he must also enter into his room to pray to the Father in secret."

One of the greatest helps to prayer is a *book of prayers.* It provides a precious treasury of words in which we can approach God every day. These ready-made prayers imprint on our minds the sentiments that the Church of Christ wants us to have in any situation.

At the same time, such prayers also give us a deeper knowledge and understanding of the Church's teaching— about God the Father, God the Son, and God the Holy Spirit. They enable us to get closer to God and to know Him better day by day.

We can, of course, also pray in our own words instead of words found on a printed page. However, many of us do not know what to say. We need help in speaking to God. As Catholics, we also need to pray in words that have been either composed by the Church or approved by her shepherds.

This new and different prayerbook is offered as an aid to help young Catholics pray. It combines the best features of both traditional prayers and contemporary prayers. In this sense, it presents prayers that are alive and vital to us, prayers that fit neatly into our daily lives—it provides *living prayers.*

No effort has been spared to insure that this book will be easy to use and most attractive to the person praying. The text is printed in large pleasing typeface and in red and black. The inspiring two-colored illustrations will help our minds to be set on Jesus and through Him on the other Persons of the Blessed Trinity.

It is the Publishers' hope that all who use this new book of prayers will achieve a deeper and more living spiritual life. May it lead them ever closer to the beatific union with the living God.

At the wedding feast of Cana, Jesus performed His first miracle through Mary's prayer. We make use of General Prayers to ask Jesus and Mary to help us in all our needs.

8

GENERAL PRAYERS

The Sign of the Cross

In the Name of the Father
and of the Son
and of the Holy Spirit. Amen.

The Glory Be

Glory be to the Father
and to the Son
and to the Holy Spirit.
As it was in the beginning,
is now and ever shall be,
world without end. Amen.

The Divine Blessing

May almighty God bless us:
the Father and the Son and the Holy
  Spirit. Amen.

The Our Father

Our Father, Who art in heaven,
hallowed be Thy name.
Thy kingdom come.
Thy will be done on earth as it is in
  heaven.
Give us this day our daily bread;
and forgive us our trespasses

as we forgive those who trespass against
  us;
and lead us not into temptation,
but deliver us from evil.
For the kingdom and the power and the
  glory
are Yours, now and forever. Amen.

The Gloria

Glory to God in the highest,
and peace to His people on earth.
Lord God, heavenly King,
almighty God and Father,
  we worship You, we give You thanks,
  we praise You for Your glory.
Lord Jesus Christ, only Son of the Father,
Lord God, Lamb of God,
You take away the sin of the world:
  have mercy on us;
You are seated at the right hand of the
    Father:
  receive our prayer.
For You alone are the Holy One,
You alone are the Lord,
You alone are the Most High,
  Jesus Christ,
  with the Holy Spirit,
  in the glory of God the Father. Amen.

The Doxology

Through Him,
with Him,
in Him,
in the unity of the Holy Spirit,
all glory and honor is Yours,
almighty Father,
for ever and ever. Amen.

Holy, Holy, Holy

Holy, holy, holy Lord,
God of power and might,
heaven and earth are filled
with Your glory.
Hosanna in the highest.
Blessed is He Who comes
in the name of the Lord.
Hosanna in the highest.

Angel of God

Angel of God, my guardian dear,
to whom His love commits me here,
ever this day be at my side,
to enlighten and guard,
to rule and guide. Amen.

Lamb of God

Lamb of God,
You take away the sins of the world:
Have mercy on us
and give us Your peace.

Anima Christi (Soul of Christ)

Soul of Christ, sanctify me.
Body of Christ, save me.
Blood of Christ, inebriate me.
Water from the side of Christ, cleanse me.
Passion of Christ, strengthen me.
O good Jesus, hear me.
Within Your wounds, hide me.
Never let me be separated from You.
From the malignant enemy, protect me.
At the hour of my death, call me
and bid me come to You
that with Your saints I may praise You
forever and ever. Amen.

Aaronite Blessing

May the Lord bless and protect us.
May He turn His face to us and have
    mercy on us.
May His face shine on us,
and give us His peace.

Prayer of St. Francis

Lord, make me an instrument of Your
  peace.
Where there is hatred, let me sow love.
Where there is injury, let me sow pardon.
Where there is friction, let me sow union.
Where there is error, let me sow truth.
Where there is doubt, let me sow faith.
Where there is despair, let me sow hope.
Where there is darkness, let me sow light.
Where there is sadness, let me sow joy.

O Divine Master,
grant that I may not so much seek
to be consoled as to console,
to be understood as to understand,
to be loved as to love.
For it is in giving that we receive.
It is in pardoning that we are pardoned.
It is in dying that we are born to eternal
  life.

For the Dead

Eternal rest grant to the deceased,
O Lord,
and let perpetual light shine upon them.
May they rest in peace. Amen.
May their souls and the souls
of the all faithful departed through the
mercy of God rest in peace. Amen.

Hail, Mary

Hail, Mary, full of grace,
the Lord is with you;
blessed are you among women
and blessed is the fruit of your womb,
  Jesus.
Holy Mary, Mother of God
pray for us sinners,
now and at the hour of our death. Amen.

Hail, Holy Queen

Hail, holy Queen, Mother of mercy;
hail, our life, our sweetness, and our hope.
To you do we cry,
poor banished children of Eve.
To you do we send up our sighs,
mourning and weeping in this valley of
  tears.
Turn then, most gracious Advocate,
your eyes of mercy toward us.
And after this our exile
show unto us the blessed fruit of your
  womb, Jesus.
O clement, O loving, O sweet Virgin
  Mary.

Remember, O Most Gracious Virgin Mary

Remember, O most gracious Virgin Mary,
that never was it known
that anyone who fled to your protection,
implored your help or sought your intercession,
was left unaided.

Inspired with this confidence,
I fly to you, O Virgin of virgins, my Mother;
to you do I come,
before you I stand, sinful and sorrowful.
O Mother of the Word Incarnate,
despise not my petitions,
but in your mercy hear and answer me.
Amen.

The Second Person of the Trinity became man and began a new day of salvation for us. So we begin each new day with prayer that we may attain His salvation.

WHEN I AWAKE

A New Day

My God, You have during this night
watched over me like a father from above.
I praise and glorify You in day's light,
and thank You for Your blessed love.

Father, direct and bless today
whatever I think, and do, and say.
Protect me from all sin and evil,
from pain and death and other trouble.

Bless me, too, I do implore,
O Holy Angel of God, my Lord.
Mary, my mother, at God's throne
pray for me with Jesus, your Son,
Who is forever highly praised
for all time in joyful ways.

How happy I awake in morning light.
How well have I slept this peaceful night.
Thanks to You, my heavenly Father,
for being with me through nighttime
    slumber.
Stay with me also this new day
so that no suffering will come my way.

For Help

Dear God, help me today,
to do Your will, I sincerely pray!

My Day

I have awakened healthy.
Thank You, dear God of all.
Today keep me good and happy.
Protect everyone, great and small.

I Open My Eyes

I open my eyes and look to You, O God.
You have watched over my sleep and
    kept nighttime guard.
Protect me today, too, is my humble plea
so that no harm can come to me.

The Day Begins

Good Father, the day begins.
Touch us all, each of Your children,
that at play and serious actions,
we may give joy to You and to our
    parents.

Blessings

Father, bless me today.
Bless my heart.
Bless my dear parents,
and my brothers and sisters.
Bless those who are related to us.
Bless all people in the nation.
Bless us in all things,
so that we may attain heaven
in fulfillment of Your wishes.

Guide Me

Dear God, I ask You,
guide me this day new,
that what I think, say, and do,
may have Your blessing, too.

For Today

Dear Father in heaven,
speak Your blessing over me,
so that I may begin and end
the new day well.

The New Day Dawns

The new day dawns,
the night is now past.
Lord, in all that I do
I want to start my day with You,
to help all life
love peace, not strife.
On all good actions,
Lord, help with Your blessings.

Sunrise

When the sun has risen
and the day has begun,
I praise God in heaven
with a heart full of joy.

Thank You

I have awakened today
in morning's light.
Thank You for staying with me
through this dark night.

Before I Go Out

Dear Father,
before I go out today
for Your blessing, I earnestly pray.
Spread out Your hands and in Your care
lead me on Your paths so fair.

Your Blessing

Father in heaven,
look upon us and bless us.
Bless also those we meet today,
and lead us on the proper way,
that we may do good and find You.

Father in Heaven

Father in heaven,
have mercy on us and bless us.
We worship You, O holy God.
We venerate You and love You.
Show us today the correct way.
Help us do what You want,
to be as You want us to be,
and to praise and glorify You
now and for all eternity.

On Our Way

Lord, let us go on our way today
with Your guidance and without hin-
   drance,
and let us stand everywhere in Your grace
to thank You, Lord, and give You praise.

Thanks for a New Day

Father in heaven, we thank You
for bringing us to this day.
We are glad that we may experience it.
You make us happy.
You give us what we need.
Don't abandon us this day.
Make our hearts good so that we seek
   You.
We praise and glorify You.
We thank You for everything.

Stay With Us

Dear Father in heaven,
we are grateful to You for our sleep this
    night.
Now You are calling us into this day.
Stay with us when we play and are happy,
when we are in danger and alone,
when we should avoid evil and do good.

Stay always with all
who especially need Your help today,
who are poor or sick or sad.
You love everyone, so bless us all.
In the name of the Father and of the Son
and of the Holy Spirit we want to begin
    this day.

Beginning the Day

Lord, almighty God,
You have let us reach the beginning of
    this day;
protect us today by Your strength.
Don't let us fall into any sin today;
instead, let our thoughts, words, and
    actions
be constantly directed to what is right,
so that we may offer our day to You.
Through Christ our Lord.

Direct Our Day

The rays of the sun are already bright
and so we implore You in day's light
to keep us in all our activity
free from sin and pain today.

Put a bridle on our tongue
so that it can never begin strife,
and shield our eyes
especially from worthless sights.

Keep our hearts pure
and free from all anger.
Help us control the desire of our senses
with proper measure in food and drink,

That, when the day is done
and the night embraces us kindly,
we, happy and pure because of our re-
    straint,
will dedicate our song of thanks to You,
    our God.

Praise be to the Father on His throne,
and His only-begotten Son.
Also to the Holy Spirit constantly
from now through all eternity.

You Have Given Us Light

We praise You, Lord Jesus Christ,
because it has now become day
and You have given us light.
Give us also the grace and power
to live this, Your day,
according to Your will.

Offering

The day, Lord God, has dawned anew.
I praise and thank You faithfully.
Today, my Lord, I begin with You
ready for service and Your use of me.

I want to offer to You this day:
my words, my thoughts, and all my
    actions,
everything that I do and say,
my work, my rest, my recreation.

I give to You for overseeing
my heart, my soul, my entire being.

In Our Midst

You, O Lord, are in our midst,
and in Your holy Name we pray:
Do not abandon us today.

Bless Me

May God the Father, Son, and Holy
   Spirit
 bless me now.
Lord, make all that I encounter today
   proceed according to Your will.
Let whatever happens give glory to Your
   Name.
I want only to increase Your praise
   and extol Your goodness.

Before retiring for the night, Jesus spent much time in prayer to His Father. At the end of the day, we too spend time in loving conversation with God our Father.

WHEN I SLEEP

At Day's End

Lord, the day has now come to an end.
Thankfully I begin my rest.
You alone can all gifts send:
Protect my sleep and let me be blest.

For Sleep

I want to fall asleep tonight;
please give me, O Jesus, Your blessing,
that I may peacefully rest in Your loving
  light
till morning's new day unfolding.

Guard Me Tonight

God, You have protected me today;
guard me this night, too.
I'm happy to fall asleep aware
that we are always in Your care.

I Am Tired

I am tired.
I close my eyes.
Father, watch over me
as I lie in bed.

Forgive Me

If I have done wrong today,
Forgive me, dear God, I pray.
Your grace and Jesus' blood
Cleanse us, making all harm good.

For Relatives

God, take all who are related to me
and keep them in Your sight.
All persons, great and small,
are commended to You tonight.

For Sick Hearts

Send peace to sick hearts,
close crying eyes.
With the moon high above us,
watch over the still world.

For a Restful Night

All-powerful God,
grant what I now ask.
Protect my life this night.
Help me rest well and safely.
Look down from heaven
upon my dear parents, too.
Tomorrow, let us all be happy again
and faithfully thankful to You.

Before the Day Ends

Before the day ends,
my night prayers I will say.
For all His gifts, I thank God
—for the blessings He sent my way.

And for this night I will now ask
that He guard me in my sleep,
that no bad dream will awaken me,
and that I not fear the darkness deep.

Help me to awake happy when
bright morning's sunshine comes again.

Today Was Such a Beautiful Day

Today was such a beautiful day, dear God,
and it has again brought me so much joy.
Gratefully I say good night;
have mercy on us all.

Remember the poor,
and protect my parents, too.
Help us fall asleep peacefully.

Soon I Will Sleep

Dear God, soon I will sleep.
Tonight send Your holy angels
to watch over me, please.
Protect all whom I love;
forgive all my sins.
Let me be happy when the sun rises
   above.

Tonight

Father in heaven,
we thank You
   for having given us this day.

Please forgive us
   for any wrongdoing.
Protect us tonight
   when darkness is upon us.

Send Your holy angels
   to protect us.

Please help others, too:
   Comfort the sad;
   help the sick;
   have mercy on the abandoned;
   and touch the hardhearted.

Have a Good Night

Now, have a good night, brothers and
  sisters.
The Lord in heaven is watching
and in His goodness He wants to protect
  us.

Your Love

Dear Father in heaven,
You love us always and faithfully.
We have experienced Your love today.
Again we have so much reason to thank
  You.

Forgive us, if today we have not been
as You actually wanted us to be.
We believe and trust
that You will watch over us when we
  sleep.

We ask You to protect us,
our families, our neighbors, and all
  persons.
May Your blessing always be upon us.

In the name of the Father
and of the Son
and of the Holy Spirit
we want to end this day.

Thank You for Today

Dear God and Father,
we do now what we do every evening:
We thank You for this day.
You have given it to us.
You have called us.
We thank You for every joy,
for all persons who were good to us,
and we especially thank You for loving us.

We are sorry for whatever
we have not done well today.
Forgive us for the times
we were not nice and good,
we were naughty, disrespectful, and
    ungrateful,
we annoyed others, and
we were unfriendly and quarrelsome.
Help us do better tomorrow.

Now we ask You for a good night
for ourselves, this home, our parents,
brothers, sisters, and friends near and far.
We pray especially for the people
who are suffering and are in need.
Bless us all.

Bless Us All

Lord, help those who die tonight
and lead us all into Your heavenly light.
I thank You for all that was beautiful
   today,
for what I could do and for those You
   sent my way.

I thank You for all those who love me,
for my parents, brothers, sisters, and
   friends.
Help me to be grateful.

I ask Your forgiveness for everything
that was not right and good today:
when I harmed others;
when I angered them;
when I avoided work instead of helping.

I am sorry for my mistakes.
I want to do better tomorrow.

Thank You for loving me just as I am.
I pray for all who are unhappy,
who suffer need, who hunger, who are
   lonesome,
and for the sick and the dying.
Help them and show me how I, too,
   can help them.

Lord, bless us all
and give us all a peaceful night.

We Praise You, Father

P. = Parent or Leader   C. = Child

P. Father in heaven,
We want to praise and honor You tonight.

C. *You .are close to us and make our hearts light.*

P. We thank You for what we have:

C. *We have a home.*

P. We have clothes.

C. *We have toys.*

P. We have each other,

C. *father, mother, sister, and brother.*

P. We ask You for good and restful slumber

C. *for ourselves, our friends, and all our neighbors,*

P. but also for those who are in need

C. *of a bed to sleep and food to eat,*

P. for those who are alone and scared

C. *whom no one loves, and for whom no one cares.*

P. Help them all overcome their misery.

C. *Grant us all life with You eternally.*

Evening Song

Now we want to sing the evening song
and pray that God will protect us.
Though many eyes cry every night
until the sun awakens in the morning
and many stars, indeed, shine every night,
the Lord God in heaven keeps watch.

Before Daylight Dims

P. = Parent or Leader   C. = Child

P. Before daylight dims, Lord,
   hear this prayer:

C. *You are so gentle and so good;*
   take us mercifully under Your care.

P. Grant that no evil dream awakens us,
   and that no nightmare frightens us.

C. *Hold back evil's tempting allure*
   so that we may always remain pure.

P. Hear us, gentle Father, Who, with
      Your Son,
   the loving image of Your perfection,

C. *and with the Spirit, everlasting*
      Consoler,
   will live and reign forever and ever.
      Amen.

Bless This House

We ask You, Lord, to bless this house.
Keep all evil far from it.
Let Your holy angels live in it
so that they may protect us in peace.
May Your blessing be over us for all time
Through Christ our Lord.

This Night

In this night, O God, protect and guard
    me.
By Your power, keep me safe from sin
    and pain
and from Satan's cunning and envy.
Help me in the last battle, in the dangers
    of death.

O my Jesus, Your holy wounds
should be a resting place for my soul.
Close my eyes in peace.
I give myself completely to You.

O great Lady, Mary, hear me;
during my sleep I entrust my heart to you.
St. Joseph, too, protect me like a father.
Guardian Angel, help me by your prayers.

Moonrise

The moon has risen and in heaven
golden stars glitter bright and clear.
The forest stands dark and silent,
and from the meadows the fog lifts won-
    drously.

How still is the world
and, in the veil of twilight,
so snug and so charming—
like a still room
where you fall asleep
and forget this day's worry.

God, let Your salvation renew us;
let us not build on anything mortal;
let us not enjoy vanity.
Let us become innocent, pious, and
    happy,
like children before You here on earth.

In Your time, take us from this world
by an easy death and let no one sorrow.
And when You have taken us, lead us to
    heaven,
we ask You, our Lord and our God.

So, then, we all lie down in God's name;
the evening breeze is cold.
Spare us, God, punishment
and let us sleep quietly—
and our sick neighbors, too.

When a storm arose on the sea, Jesus calmed the waves and kept the disciples from drowning. In the storms of life, we have recourse to Jesus to keep us safe and lead us to salvation.

I NEED YOU, LORD

Listen to Me, Please

Listen to me, please, O Lord.
Protect me, for I am devoted to You.
You are my God!
Gladden my soul for You are so good and
forgiving.
I give thanks to You, O Lord my God,
with all my heart,
because You have helped and comforted
me.

According to Psalm 86

My Guardian

When I am sad and alone,
who will help me then?
Help will come to me from God;
He has made heaven and earth.
He does not doze or sleep;
God is always with me, day and night.
He protects me from all evil;
God protects my life!
God protects my coming and going
every day anew!

Adapted from Psalm 121

I Am Sick

Dear God, I am sick.
I have slept badly.
And now I cannot go out
to the other children.
I ache. Food does not taste good.
But You don't want me to be sad.
Help me be patient,
and be well again soon.
Make me grateful to all who help me.

Our Help

Lord, give us a big heart for all persons.
Lord, help us to see You!
Lord, help us to love You!
Lord, lead us and strengthen us!
Savior of the world,
come and make us all happy.

We Want You

We want to listen to You.
We want to believe in You.
We want to love You.
Lead us all into Your heavenly kingdom.

I Am Sad, Lord

Dear Lord Jesus Christ, Savior of the World,
Friend of all persons,
I am so sad and do not really know why.
  (Or: because I have not gotten my way;
  because I am sick;
  because I have hurt myself;
  because I have done wrong . . .)
You are always with me and care for me.
You do not want me to be sad.
You have borne the Cross.
I want to overcome my pain because I love You.
Help me that I may again be happy and make others happy.

Easter Light

We love You, Lord Jesus Christ,
because You are our Friend and Brother
and have given us the Easter light.
Give us also Your strength today,
which brings about and creates goodness in us,
so that we may live according to Your will.

Lead Me, Lord

I thank You, Lord Jesus Christ,
Creator of the world.
When, in time, You come with power and
glory,
You will completely destroy the power of
evil.
Whoever serve You can rejoice,
for they will enter eternal life.

Therefore, lead me, Lord Jesus Christ,
You, Who are my Lord and Savior.
Let me be faithfully devoted to You;
make my faith strong and pure.

Jesus, Help Me Be Like You

Jesus, I want to be like You,
and please You in all I do.
Give me Your grace to help me
to live as You lived,
and to keep from every sin.
I give You my heart in truest love
and want to serve You faithfully,
because You have done so much for me,
and given Your Heart to me.

We Believe

Father in heaven, we believe in You.
You love us so much,
that You sent Jesus to us on earth.
Born in Bethlehem, He came to us.
When He grew up, He helped many.
He said, God loves you and all persons.

But the people wanted to go their own
   way.
They did not want to hear
the happy message of Jesus.
Indeed, they persecuted and killed Him.

You, however, heavenly Father,
are stronger and more powerful than we.
You have again made Jesus live.
We especially think about this every
   Sunday.

Father, we are happy that You
are close to us with Jesus Christ,
the Savior of the world, our Friend.
We thank You for having called us
to be eternally joined with You in heaven
in the days to come.

Protect Me

Let me happily wander homeward
without trouble and fear.
Protect me, protect the others,
heavenly Father, dear.

Before Going to School

St. Raphael with Tobiah,
St. Gabriel with Mary,
St. Michael with the heavenly host,
be a protection and a defense for us
on our way to school.

Comfort Us

Dear Father in heaven,
You have sent us Your Son as Savior.
When there is need and pain,
You come to help us.
Console the sick,
and make them healthy soon.

Comfort them in their illness.
Give them strength and trust in You,
so that they may patiently endure their
    sufferings.
Show them the Cross of Your Son
and prepare them to bear their pain
out of love for Him.

In My Distress

O Lord, hear my prayer
in the time of my distress.
You, O Lord, abide forever.
Look down from Your holy place
and answer me speedily.

Adapted from Psalm 102

For the Departed

Lord, have mercy
on our departed brothers and sisters
and all who have fallen asleep in Your
peace.
Take them up into Your glory.

In Sickness

The Lord will help me in my sickness.
I will call upon Him:
Have pity on me; heal me.

Adapted from Psalm 41

We Remember the Dead

Dear Father in heaven,
You will that all persons be eternally
    happy
and blessed with You.
We remember the dead and implore You,
take them up into Your peace.

We especially pray to You for
those who die suddenly,
those who die of starvation,
those who are killed daily on the roads,
those who commit suicide.

Be merciful to all and console those
who have become lonely and sad
because of a death.

Lord, Have Mercy on Us

Heavenly Father,
have mercy on our dearly departed.
Take them, and all who have died, into
    Your peace.
Give them Your light
through our Lord Jesus Christ.

For Eternal Peace

Dear Father in heaven,
every day You bring people
into Your holy and beautiful kingdom.
We say, "They have died,"
or "They have gone home to You."

Many were previously sick;
many died suddenly on the roads;
many died unexpectedly, old or young;
many have become old and tired.
We pray to You for them all.
Let them find an eternal home
and eternal peace with You.

We pray to You, also,
for those who have remained behind:
For the children who no longer have a
    mother or a father;
for the parents who had to lose a child;
for the mother who no longer has a hus-
    band;
for the father who has remained alone as
    a widower.
You love them, too.
Remain with them and help them.

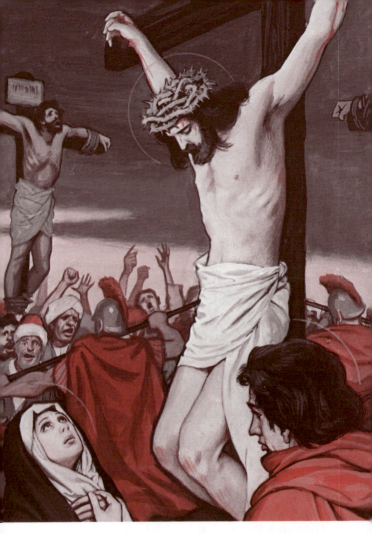

Sin is the greatest evil in the world. Jesus died on the Cross to obtain forgiveness of our sins. We ask God for pardon and strive to do better in the future.

I'M SORRY, LORD

Guide and Forgive Us

Dear Father in heaven,
You are always good to us.
We are happy that You
are always present and love us.

Guide us on the path which leads to You,
where You are always with us,
for sometimes we are not
as You want us to be.
Now we must think about and recall
what we have not done correctly.

Then we want to ask for forgiveness.
You see everything that we do.
You hear everything that we say.
You know everything that we think.
We are often so forgetful.

In the evening we no longer remember
what we have said and done during the
    day
and what was wrong in Your eyes.
Help us so that we may not be
separated from You.

You Know

You know, Lord,
   if we are envious today;
   if we wanted to have something that
      did not belong to us;
   if we begrudged others something;
   if we broke something in anger;
   if we lied;
   if we played unfairly;
   if we did not want to confess our
      wrongs;
   if we kept silent when we should have
      spoken;
   if we said something that we should
      not have said;
   if we hurt someone in the family or at
      play;
   if we tormented or laughed at someone.
You know it.

Because I love You, I want to take my-
      self in hand:
   I want to pray well;
   I want to bring joy to my father and
      mother;
   I want to do what they tell me;
   I do not want to lie;
   I do not want to quarrel;

I do not want to be a poor sport;
I want to help where I can.

Hear me, Lord, and forgive me my sins.
Help us all to stay very near to You
and to be Your children, too.
We thank You for loving us.
Convert all the sinners in the world.

Inspire me, Holy Spirit,
that I may think what is holy.
Use me, Holy Spirit,
that I may do what is holy.
Entice me, Holy Spirit,
that I may love what is holy.
Strengthen me, Holy Spirit,
that I may protect what is holy.
Keep me, Holy Spirit,
that I may never lose what is holy.

Jesus is the Good Shepherd Who takes special care of all His sheep. We pray to Him to guard and keep us always close to Him.

52

STAY WITH ME, LORD

Wherever I Go

Wherever I go, wherever I stand,
You, dear God, are near at hand.
Even if I see You never,
I surely know You are with me ever.

Stay, Jesus

Jesus, stay in my soul;
keep me free from sin.
Help me choose good above all,
to be happy with You from now on.
Your care guards and protects me
from sin, danger and misery.

The Lord Is My Shepherd

The Lord is my shepherd; I shall not
want.
In verdant pastures He gives me repose;
Beside restful waters He leads me;
He refreshes my soul.
He guides me in right paths
for His name's sake.
Even though I walk in the dark valley
I fear no evil; for You are at my side
With Your rod and Your staff
that give me courage.   Psalm 23:1-4

53

Jesus, Come to Me

Jesus, I love You
in Holy Communion
when You give me
Your Body and Blood
as Food for my soul.

Come to me, Jesus,
and stay with me.
Jesus, bless our family.

Give us Your grace
to help us to be good
and to stay away from evil.

May we receive You
in Holy Communion
every time we go to Holy Mass.

Jesus, be our best Friend
and take us to heaven someday,
where we shall always be with You.

Stay by Me

Dear God, I humbly pray,
stay by me and protect me today.

Take Us by the Hand

Stay with us, God,
and bless us.
Come to us
and take us by the hand.

Adapted from Psalm 67

Jesus often expressed praise and thanks to the Father. We offer thanks to the Father at meals and for all wonderful gifts He bestows on us each day.

THANK YOU, LORD

Before Meals

Everyone awaits You, Lord.
You give food at the proper time.
You open Your hand and fill every
  living thing with blessings.

Bless us, O Lord, and these Your gifts,
which we are about to receive from Your
  goodness
through Christ our Lord.

May the King of eternal glory lead us
to the feast of eternal glory. Amen.

Before Meals

Come, Lord Jesus, be our guest.
Let what You have prepared for us be
  blest.

Before Meals

Every gift comes from You.
Whatever we need, You give.
To You all praise and glory, too.
Our thanks for helping us live.

After Meals

We thank You, almighty God,
for all Your gifts,
You, Who live and reign forever and
ever. Amen.

Lord, reward all who do good to us
for the sake of Your name.
Give them eternal life. Amen.

After Meals

We thank You, Lord Jesus Christ.
You have been our guest.
With You here with us, we have no need.
For You are truly heaven's bread.

After Meals

God is great,
God is good.
We thank Him
for His gifts.

The Crucifix

We thank You, Lord Jesus,
for the blood You have shed.
Let Your agonizing death for us
not be squandered or wasted.

Thank You, God

You, great God, have heard us.
Your goodness has richly rewarded us.
To You all our thanks
for all of our days.
From the bottom of our hearts,
all honor and praise.

Thanks for My Country

Lord God, I give You thanks
for letting me live
in this great land
which is filled with good things.

Thank You for letting me be free
to live in peace
and to worship You without fear.

Help all the citizens of our country
to follow Your holy Will
and to live in love for each other
and for You.

Gifts

All good gifts
come from the Lord God.
Therefore, thank Him and hope in Him.

Creation

Father in heaven,
we thank You for being a good Father to
us.
You have wondrously made everything:
Persons and animals,
the air and the birds,
the earth and the waters.
Thus we thank You
for the flowers and trees,
for the birds and fishes.

You have given us the power
to create and work.
Thus we thank You
for the houses and factories,
for the streets and cars,
for the machines and airplanes.
You care for us, too, in everything that
happens.

Thanks, good Father, for all Your gifts,
especially for those who are good to us
and who care for us every day.

For Myself

Dear Father in heaven,
I thank You for everything
that You have given me.
I have a father and mother
(brothers and sisters).
I have enough to eat and drink.
I can sing and play.
I can run and jump.
I can see and hear.
You love me.
I am happy.
And even if I am sad,
I do not want to stop thanking You.
I thank You for everything.

You Know Me

God, You know me so well!
You know when I am awake and when I
  sleep,
when I work and when I play;
God, You know me so well!

You have formed my inmost being;
You knit me in my mother's womb.
Thank You very much, O great God,
for I am wonderfully made.

Adapted from Psalm 139

You Are Very Close

Dear God, You are not only
above the clouds and stars,
but You are everywhere.
You are very close to us wherever we are:
At home or in the garden or on the street,
whether we are playing, lying in bed, or
    asleep.

You are also near to us whenever we pray,
whenever we hear stories
about the Savior of the world
or whenever we are in church.
You are in our hearts
although hidden from our eyes.
Therefore, we have no fear,
for we know for sure that You love us.

Because You love us, we all belong to-
    gether.
You keep us together
even if we disagree with each other.
All persons in the whole world belong to-
    gether.
If they desire it, they may belong
to the family of God
and are His children.
Dear God, Father of all, we thank You.

Hymn of Thanksgiving

P. = Parent or Leader   C. = Child

P.   Thank God, for He is good.

C.   *He loves us always!*

P.   He has made the earth so beautiful.

C.   *He loves us always!*

P.   He has made the sun and moon.

C.   *He loves us always!*

P.   God helps our mother who cares for
us.

C.   *He loves us always!*

P.   God helps our father in his work!

C.   *He loves us always!*

P.   God is good to all.

C.   *He loves us always!*

Adapted from Psalm 136

The Lord Will Come

See, the Lord will come,
and with Him all His saints.
On that day, a bright light
will shine. Alleluia.

After seeing the Risen Jesus, St. Thomas exclaimed, "My Lord and my God." We praise God for this tremendous miracle and for all other great deeds He has done for us.

I PRAISE YOU, LORD

Praised Be God

Praised be God, the powerful Father.
Praised be His faithfulness.
He gives us a good night.
He gives us another day.
Father, let Your blessing rest on me,
for all my days.
And teach me to do good,
to do Your will.

Praise Him

Let all who honor Him,
praise the Lord.
Let us sing His name with happiness,
And bring praise and thanks to His altar.
Praise the Lord for His loving faithfulness.

I Praise You, Lord

Lord, You are good.
Lord, You are great.
Lord, You are beautiful.
Lord, You are strong.
You are the King of the whole world.
Lord, You are close to me.
Lord Jesus, always stay with me.
I want to be Your friend.
Alleluia.

Dear Lord

Dear Lord, Jesus,
Son of the living God,
You became man for us.
You are the Savior of the world.
You died on the Cross for us.
You rose from the dead.
You went up into heaven, Jesus.
You are our heavenly Lord.

Praise and Honor

Most Holy Lord Jesus,
Lord of all lords,
Son of God and Mary,
I want to love You.
I want to honor You,
Joy and crown of my soul.

All the beauty of heaven and earth
is joined in You alone.
No one should ever become dearer to me
than You, my dear Jesus.

Your Holy Cross

Lord Jesus Christ,
we pray to You and praise You,
for through Your holy Cross
You have redeemed the world.

Praise and Glory

Lord, You have given us:
health and a happy life,
two eyes to see Your world,
and a heart to understand Your word.
So, my words will praise You eternally.
Creator above, for Your glory
I praise Your holy name,
for now and for all time. Amen.

Great God

Whatever I have, comes from You.
Whatever I need, You give me.
Whatever I see, beckons me.
God, how great, how good You are!

All Are Yours

No animal on earth
is too small for You, dear God.
You let them all exist,
and they are all Yours.
To You, all life cries out.
The birds sing to You,
the fish jump for You,
the bees buzz for You,
the beetles hum for You,
the little mice squeak for You.
Lord God, You are to be praised.

Creator, We Praise You

P. = Parent or Leader   C. = Child

P.   The heavens, they are so high,
           the sun, how it shines in the sky,
           and the stars, they twinkle in the
               blue,
           Creator, they all praise You.

P. & C.   *Yes, we praise and glorify the Lord.*

C.   The winds, they blow and scurry,
           the thunder rolls in fury,
           and the lightning flashes in view.
           Creator, they all praise You.

P. & C.   *Yes, we praise and glorify the Lord.*

P.   The birds, they sing songs sweet,
           the fish swim far and deep,
           and the animals leap the day
               through.
           Creator, they all praise You.

P. & C.   *Yes, we praise and glorify the Lord.*

C.   The flowers, they bloom and multi-
               ply,
           the trees rustle and call to the sky,
           and everything that has breath, too,
           Creator, we all praise You.

P. & C.   *Yes, we praise and glorify the Lord.*

Let God Be Praised

Heavenly expanse of light and blue,
how many stars do you number?
  Countless! Let God
  be praised so many times!

God's well ordered world,
how many specks of dust do you number?
  Countless! Let God
  be praised so many times!

O summer field, tell us too,
how many blades of grass do you number?
  Countless! Let God
  be praised so many times!

Dark forest, well formed,
how many branches do you number?
  Countless! Let God
  be praised so many times!

Deep ocean all around,
how many drops do you number?
  Countless! Let God
  be praised so many times!

Sunshine, clear and pure,
how many rays do you number?
  Countless! Let God
  be praised so many times!

Eternity, infinite time,
how many hours do you number?
  Countless! Let God
  be praised so many times!

Praise and Glorify the Lord

Praise and glorify the Lord, you peoples,
Rejoice in Him and serve Him gladly.
All you people, praise the Lord.

Greening meadows in magnificent splen-
  dor,
proclaim the goodness and power of the
  Eternal One,
and boast of God's goodness and power.

Glory be forever to the Ruler of the world,
Who created it and keeps it mighty.
Honor to Him Whose world it is.

We Honor You

Honor and praise be
to the King of eternity,
to the immortal,
to the invisible,
to the only God,
forever and ever. Amen.

King of All

All you peoples, clap your hands,
  shout to God with cries of gladness,
For the Lord, the Most High, the awe-
    some,
  is the great king over all the earth.
Amid trumpet blasts, sing praise to our
  King.
God reigns over the nations,
  God sits upon His holy throne.

Psalm 47:1-3, 6-7, 9

Hymn of All Creation

Praise the Lord from the heavens;
  praise Him in the heights.
Praise Him, all you His angels;
  praise Him, all you His hosts.
Praise Him, sun and moon;
  praise Him, all you shining stars.
Praise Him, you highest heavens,
  and you waters above the heavens.
Let them praise the name of the Lord,
    for He commanded and they were
      created.
He established them forever and ever,
  for the Lord loves His people.
Let the faithful exult in glory;
  let them sing for joy upon their couches.
Let the high praises of God
  be in their throats.

Psalms 148—149

A Song of Praise

Great God, we praise You.
Lord, we exalt Your strength.
The earth bows before You
and admires Your works.
As You were in the beginning,
You are now, and ever shall be.

Everything that can praise You,
Cherubim and Seraphim,
join in a song of praise to You.
All the angels who serve You
call to You unceasingly,
Holy, holy, holy, Lord.

God of the heavenly hosts,
strong helper in times of need,
heaven, earth, air, and seas
are filled with Your glory.
Everything belongs to You.

Praise to God, the Creator

You are a great God!
You have made the earth and the sea,
the high mountains and the brooks in the
    valley,
from which the animals drink their fill.
Yes, You are a great God.

The birds of heaven nest in the trees,
from the branches they chirp their songs.
The goat lives on the high mountains,
the badgers run among the rocks,
the lions roar and hunt for something to
  eat.
Yes, You are a great God!

You have cared for all persons well,
have given them knowledge to sow wheat
and to harvest grains for the daily bread.
Yes, You are a great God!

You have made the moon and the beautiful sun,
the whole world belongs to You!
The sea is so great and wide,
large and small fish swim in the cool
  water,
and many ships travel from country to
  country.
Yes, You are a great God!

You give Your blessings to everything
  that lives.
I thank You, good God.

Adapted from Psalm 104

Jesus is the King of all hearts. We acknowledge His wonderful kingship over us and offer ourselves completely to Him for time and eternity.

I AM YOURS, LORD

I Trust You

Father, I trust in You.
Let my thoughts and actions
fulfill Your will, too.

Good Shepherd

Good Shepherd, You are true nourish-
ment.
Jesus, strengthen us on our journey
until we come into Your Father's kingdom.
Nourish us here in our earthly dwelling;
call us one day to the wedding feast;
make us like Your saints.

At Christmastime

I am standing here at Your manger,
O Jesus, my life.
I come to bring and to give You
what You have given me.
Take it; it is my spirit and mind,
my heart, soul, and courage.
Take it all
and let it be pleasing to You.

Lead Us, Lord

Lord God, King of heaven and earth,
today, with Your grace,
lead and sanctify, rule and guide
our hearts and bodies,
our thoughts, words, and deeds,
according to Your law,
and in fulfillment of Your command-
    ments.
Thus, with Your help
we will be blessed and free
here and in eternity,
O Savior of the world,
Who live and reign forever and ever.

Imitation

Lord, we want to imitate You,
and courageously, piously, confidently,
and gladly come to life
through our own crosses.
Whoever does not struggle,
does not wear the crown of eternal life.

You Are Risen

I am happy, Lord Jesus Christ,
that You are elevated in heaven.
A place is also prepared there for me,
to be with You forever and ever.

To Jesus in the Tabernacle

Jesus, I thank You
for Your presence in the tabernacle
day and night to be with me
and to hear my prayers
when I need Your help.

You are my best Friend.
I want to come to visit You often.
I want to show You how much I love You,
and to ask You to help me
and those I love.

O Sacrament most holy,
O Sacrament divine!
All praise and all thanksgiving
be every moment Thine!

Those dearest to us in this world are our parents, brothers and sisters, relatives, and friends. We pray for their welfare that we may also be with them in heaven.

FOR MY FAMILY AND FRIENDS

My Family

For my family,
  parents and brothers and sisters:
May the God Who created us
  bless us.
May the Son Who suffered on the Cross
  strengthen us.
May the Holy Spirit Who lives and works
    in us
  guide us.

For My Parents

I commend my parents to You;
protect them, dear God, for me.
Repay, O Lord, where I cannot,
the goodness they have done for me.
Keep them alive for a long time,
give them much good,
and at life's end,
grant them eternal bliss.

Lord, let my brothers and sisters, too,
be commended to Your protection.
You, holy angels, help them
that they may faithfully serve our dear
  God.

Protect Us

Dear God, protect my father,
my mother,
my sisters and brothers,
and all people.

Protect My Father and Mother

Dear God, I humbly ask You
to protect my father.
Whenever he does his work,
give him joy, patience, and courage.
If it pleases You, kindly protect him
today from sins and dangers.

Dear God, I ask You,
please protect my mother.
Whenever she works and cares for us,
bless, help, and strengthen her.
May You kindly protect her
today from sins and dangers.

We Are Together

Dear God, we thank You
that we are all together.
Show us, every day,
how we can make each other happy.

Help Us

Dear Father in heaven,
I thank You for my parents
and I heartily ask You
to give them health and strength
that they may care for us.
Give them patience with us
and grant us all that we need for salvation.

Help our whole family
that we may be kind and good to each
    other
just as You want us to be.
Forgive us when we are obstinate and
    unkind
and take all guilt from us.
Help us make each other happy.

Help me to be grateful.
Let me not forget
what my father and mother do for me
    daily.
Bless their works and efforts.
Also bless my brothers and sisters
and all my relatives and friends.

Let not one of us be lost
but let us all reach our heavenly goal
where we may eternally rejoice
in the communion of saints with You.

For Friends

Dear Father in heaven,
You want to make us all happy.
You do not want any strife.
It pleases You to see that we love each
    other.
You do not want anyone to be sad.
We want to try to help each other.
Guide us and help us.

We Can Play

Dear Father in heaven,
I am able to play so well.
I like to play.
That makes me happy.
I thank You for that.
When I play, I learn a lot, too.
I am surprised again and again
how beautiful Your world is.

I also have friends to play with.
I like to play with them.
I don't want to be a poor sport.
Keep us healthy and happy
and let everything happen
for Your glory and Your honor.

I Am Not Alone

Dear God, I am not alone,
for You gave me my sisters and brothers.
Help us to always share,
and to like and respect each other.
Heal whatever pains us.
And when we, indeed, go to heaven,
let us stand there together.

You Have Given Me a Family

Dear God, You have given me parents
and brothers and sisters.
I thank You for this.
Grant that we may love each other,
that there may be peace among us.
Grant that I can understand them
and that they understand me.

I pray to You for my parents,
for my brothers and sisters,
for all who love us,
for the sick and the old,
for the children who have no home,
for all children,
and all the people in the world.

The Church of Christ is worldwide and includes peoples from all nations. We pray for the Church and for the whole world—that all peoples may live in peace and well-being.

FOR ALL PEOPLE

For the Holy Church

Dear Father in heaven,
by baptism,
I have become a member of the Holy
    Church,
the great family of God.
We are all Your children.
Preserve us in Your love.

I pray to You for our bishop in . . .;
You have sent him and the other priests
    to us
so that they can proclaim to us the good
    news
and so that we may be reminded again
    and again
how You love us.
Help them in their holy ministry
so that they may be good shepherds.

Help our pastor in his daily cares for the
    parishioners,
for the important and not-so-important
    people,
for the healthy and the sick,
for the pious and the sinners.

Whenever we are gathered in the church,
    around the altar.
hear our requests which we bring before
    You
for the holy family of God and for all
    persons.
See how happily we want to praise and
    glorify You.

Strengthen also our Holy Father,
the Pope in Rome,
so that with the help of the Holy Spirit,
he may lead the Church through the
    storms of this time.

Give strength and courage
to missionaries throughout the world
so that the good news of Your kingdom
may penetrate into all parts of the world,
to all people in all lands.

Call and send new workers into Your
    vineyard:
Priests, deacons, sisters, brothers,
and other helpers for Your ministry.
We pray to You for this.

For Unity

Dear God, we pray to You
for people in all the world,
for other nations,
for other races,
for people who think differently
    and live differently.
Help us to respect, understand, and love
    each other.

Let there be no hate among nations.
Forgive all injustice.
Let wars end.
Let Your message be proclaimed every-
    where.
Give us peace.

For Peace

Dear Father in heaven, we beseech You:
Give peace to all nations on earth.
Protect Your Church in all countries.
Have mercy on those who live in sin,
    need, and misfortune.

Give joy to those who suffer and sorrow.
Give bread to those who starve.
Help those who are dying.

Also bless our fellow parishioners,
our dear parents, brothers, and sisters,
all children and teenagers,
and all who suffer from sickness,
old age, and loneliness.
Let all people into Your heavenly kingdom.
Praise and glory be Yours forever and
  ever.

A Litany

P. = Parent or Leader   C. = Child

P. Father in heaven, hear us, we pray.

C. *For our mother and father, hear us,
O Lord.*

P. For our whole family, hear us, O
Lord.

C. *For our friends, hear us, O Lord.*

P. For the healthy and the sick, hear
us, O Lord.

C. *For those living and dead, hear us,
O Lord.*

P. For those starving and suffering,
hear us, O Lord.

C. *For those seeking and struggling,
hear us, O Lord.*

P.　For the lonely and abandoned, hear us, O Lord.

C.　*For all peoples on earth, hear us, O Lord.*

P.　For peace in this world, hear us, O Lord.

C.　*For the holy Church, hear us, O Lord.*

P.　For all who have responsibility for others, hear us, O Lord.

C.　*For all children and teenagers, hear us, O Lord.*

P.　O holy God, You love all persons; help them all to be saved and to come into heaven.

P. & C.　*Praise and glory are Yours now and forever. Amen.*

After Jesus' Ascension, the Blessed Virgin Mary remained in prayer with the Apostles until the descent of the Holy Spirit. We ask her to continue to pray for us now that she is in heaven.

MARY, PRAY FOR US

Good Mother

Mary, good Mother of God,
take me into your protection like Jesus.
Protect me from horror and anger
and care for me like a mother.
Mary, with your dear child,
give us all your blessings.

Mary, My Mother

Mary, you are the Mother of the Lord.
Mary, I want to pray to you.
Mary, you are also my mother.
I place myself under your care.

Virgin Mine

Virgin, Mother of God mine,
let me be completely yours:
yours in life and death;
yours in accident, fear and need;
yours on the cross and in bitter suffering;
yours for all time and eternity.
Virgin, Mother of God mine,
let me be completely yours.

Mary, Hear Our Prayer

P. = Parent or Leader   C. = Child

P. The angel of the Lord brought Mary
the message
and she conceived of the Holy Spirit.
C. *Hail, Mary . . .*

P. Mary spoke: Lo, I am the servant of
the Lord,
be it done to me according to your
word.
C. *Hail, Mary . . .*

P. And the Word became flesh
and dwelt among us.
C. *Hail, Mary . . .*

P. Pray for us, holy Mother of God,
C. *that we may be worthy of the prom-
ises of Christ.*

P. Let us pray: We pray to You, Father:
Pour Your grace into our hearts.
Through the message of the angel
we acknowledge the incarnation of
Christ, Your Son;
through His suffering and Cross
let us reach the glory of His resurrec-
tion.
Through Christ our Lord. Amen.

We Fly to You

Under Your protection and guard
we fly, holy Mother of God.
Hear our petitions in our troubles,
and pray that we may be free from all
    dangers,
you, most glorious Blessed Virgin,
our Lady, our Intercessor, our Mediator.
Reconcile us with your Son;
recommend us to your Son;
place us before your Son.

Queen of Heaven

P. = Parent or Leader   **C. = Child**

P. Rejoice, O Queen of heaven.
C. *Rejoice, Mary.*

P. Rejoice, all pain is gone. Alleluia.
C. *Pray to God for us, Mary.*

P. You were worthy to bear Him,
C. *Rejoice, Mary.*

P. Rejoice, all pain is gone. Alleluia.
C. *Pray to God for us. Mary.*

P. You were worthy to bear Him,
    The Savior lives, Whom you bore.
        Alleluia.
C. *Pray to God for us, Mary.*

P. He is risen from the dead,
C. *Rejoice, Mary.*
P. As He said. He is the true God,
       Alleluia.
C. *Pray to God for us, Mary.*
P. Pray to God for us, so it will happen,
C. *Rejoice, Mary,*
P. that we will arise with Christ, Alleluia.
C. *Pray to God for us, Mary.*

Shield Us

P. = Parent or Leader   C. = Child

P. Mary, spread out your mantle.
       With it, cover and shield us.
       Under it, let us safely huddle,
       until all storms and strife pass.

C. *Patroness, full of goodness,*
       protect us at all times.

P. Your mantle is very wide and warm.
       It covers all of Christianity.
       It covers the wide world from storm.
       It is a refuge and a shelter from hu-
             manity.

C. *Patroness, full of goodness,*
       protect us at all times.

P. Mary, hope of Christianity,
    grant us your help for eternity;
    through your grace, show us the way,
    to preserve body and soul all our days.

C. *Patroness, full of goodness,*
    protect us at all times.